Sri Sri Paramahansa Yogananda
Gurudeva and Founder
Yogoda Satsanga Society of India/
Self-Realization Fellowship

SCIENTIFIC HEALING AFFIRMATIONS

Theory and Practice of Concentration

by

SRI SRI PARAMAHANSA

YOGANANDA

The Scientific Use of Concentration
and Affirmations for Healing Inharmonies of Body, Mind,
and Soul Through Reason, Will, Feeling, and Prayer

Yogoda Satsanga Society of India

FOUNDED 1917 BY PARAMAHANSA YOGANANDA

First Indian Hardcover Edition, 2022

An authorized publication of Yogoda Satsanga Society of India/Self-Realization Fellowship

The Yogoda Satsanga Society of India name and emblem shown above appear on all YSS books, recordings, and other publications, assuring the reader that a work originates with the society established by Sri Sri Paramahansa Yogananda and faithfully conveys his teachings.

Published in India by
YOGODA SATSANGA SOCIETY OF INDIA
Yogoda Satsanga Math
21, U. N. Mukherjee Road
Dakshineswar, Kolkata 700 076

Printed in India by
Kailash Paper Conversion Pvt. Ltd., Ranchi 834 001

ISBN 978-93-92126-11-6

Distributed by:

Manjul Publishing House

Also available from Yogoda Satsanga Society of India, Paramahansa Yogananda Path, Ranchi 834 001, Jharkhand and at Yogoda Satsanga Ashrams and Dhyana Kendras throughout India.

Dedicated to my Gurudeva,

Jnanavatar Swami Sri Yukteswar,

with love, reverence,

and devotion

The Spiritual Legacy of Sri Sri Paramahansa Yogananda

His Complete Writings, Lectures, and Informal Talks

Paramahansa Yogananda founded Yogoda Satsanga Society of India (YSS) in 1917 and Self-Realization Fellowship (SRF) in 1920 to disseminate his teachings worldwide and to preserve their purity and integrity for generations to come. A prolific writer and lecturer from his earliest years in America, he created a renowned and voluminous body of works on the yoga science of meditation, the art of balanced living, and the underlying unity of all great religions. Today this unique and far-reaching spiritual legacy lives on, inspiring millions of truth seekers all over the world.

In accord with the express wishes of the great Guru, Yogoda Satsanga Society of India / Self-Realization Fellowship has continued the ongoing task of publishing and keeping permanently in print *The Complete Works of Paramahansa Yogananda*. These include not only the final editions of all the books he published during his lifetime, but also many new titles—works that had remained unpublished at the time of his passing in 1952, or which had been serialized over the years in incomplete form in Yogoda Satsanga Society of India/ Self-Realization Fellowship's magazine, as well as hundreds of profoundly inspiring lectures and informal talks recorded but not printed before his passing.

Paramahansa Yogananda personally chose and trained those close disciples who formed the Yogoda Satsanga Society of India/Self-Realization Fellowship Publications Council, giving them specific guidelines for the preparation and publishing of his teachings. The members of the YSS/SRF Publications Council (monks and nuns who have taken lifelong vows of renunciation and selfless service) honour these guidelines as a sacred trust, in order that the universal message of this beloved world teacher will live on in its original power and authenticity.

The Yogoda Satsanga Society of India/Self-Realization Fellowship emblem (shown on previous page) was designated by Paramahansa Yogananda to identify the nonprofit society he founded as the authorized source of his teachings. The YSS/SRF name and emblem appear on all YSS/SRF publications and recordings, assuring the reader that a work originates with the organization founded by Paramahansa Yogananda and conveys his teachings as he himself intended they be given.

—Yogoda Satsanga Society of India/ Self-Realization Fellowship

Contents

Part II
Method of Practice

Preface

From the embryonic period of man's reason he has sought to understand the mysteries of his existence and the nature of his Creator. Enlightenment on these matters has been the special mission of wise men in every age. Realizing this, the ideal of *satsanga* (company with the good and the wise) has rooted itself in the very core of India's spiritual tradition. From *satsanga* the *sadhak* gathers inspiration and advances his spiritual understanding. The more divine the good company is, the more the *sadhak* can absorb from the experience. But only a fortunate few have the rare and blessed opportunity to be actually in the personal company of a truly great soul. The seeking masses are denied this privilege if we take literally the concept of *satsanga* as the necessity to be in the physical presence of the saint. If, however, we realise that the intrinsic value of *satsanga* is in the ability of the devotee to be receptive to the teachings and guidance of the saint, whether or not the *sadhak* be in the physical company of that divine soul, the modern medium of the printed word brings the upliftment of *satsanga* to the *sadhana* of every seeker.

It is in this spirit that *Scientific Healing Affirmations* is offered to the reader.

His Holiness Sri Sri Paramahansa Yogananda, who speaks to you in the pages of this booklet, entered mahasamadhi on March 7, 1952. The remarkable incorruptibility of his body after death was a continued reflection of his unique, spiritually transcendent life. He is the revered Guru-founder of the now worldwide institution of Yogoda Satsanga Society of India/Self-Realization Fellowship. The basis of his teaching is *Raja Yoga,* the ancient, universal science of soul-realization. The Society carries on its activities and spreads the teachings of Sri Sri Paramahansa Yogananda through publication of his books and writings, including confidential spiritual lessons; and through the medium of branch centres, and educational and charitable institutions. If this booklet is the reader's first introduction to Sri Sri Paramahansa Yogananda and the Society he founded, the experience of *satsanga* with the blessed Guru in these pages may well be the beginning of a deeper acquaintance and continuing relationship.

The worth of any writing consists in its ability to convey the intended message; the authority of the message lies in the qualifications of the writer. The contents of this booklet will speak for itself; the authority of the author is readily confirmed by a thoughtful perusal of *Autobiography of a Yogi,* the life testimony of one to whom Truth was not fact but realization.

Yogoda Satsanga Society of India

PART I

Theory of Healing

1
Why Affirmations Work

Man's word is spirit in man. Spoken words are sounds occasioned by the vibrations of thoughts; thoughts are vibrations sent forth by the ego or by the soul. Every word you utter should be potent with soul vibration. A man's words are lifeless if he fails to impregnate them with spiritual force. Talkativeness, exaggeration, or falsehood makes your words as ineffective as paper bullets shot from a toy gun. The speech and prayers of garrulous or inaccurate persons are unlikely to produce beneficial changes in the order of things. Man's words should represent not only truth but also his definite understanding and realization. Speech without soul force is like husks without corn.

Spiritual Power in Man's Word

Words saturated with sincerity, conviction, faith, and intuition are like highly explosive vibration bombs, which, when set off, shatter the rocks of difficulties and create the change desired. Avoid speaking unpleasant words, even if true. Sincere words or affirmations repeated understandingly, feelingly, and willingly are sure to move the Omnipresent Cosmic Vibratory Force to render aid in your difficulty. Appeal to that Power with infinite confidence, casting out all doubt; otherwise the arrow of your attention will be deflected from its mark.

After you have sown in the soil of Cosmic

Consciousness your vibratory prayer-seed, do not pluck it out frequently to see whether or not it has germinated. Give the divine forces a chance to work uninterruptedly.

The God-Given Power of Man

Nothing is greater than Cosmic Consciousness, or God. His power far surpasses that of the human mind. Seek His aid alone. But this counsel does not mean that you should make yourself passive, inert, or credulous; or that you should minimize the power of your own mind. The Lord helps those who help themselves. He gave you will power, concentration, faith, reason, and common sense to use when trying to rid yourself of bodily and mental afflictions; you should employ all those powers while simultaneously appealing to Him.

As you utter prayers or affirmations, always believe that you are using *your own* but *God-given* powers to heal yourself or others. Ask His aid; but realize that you yourself, as His beloved child, are employing His gifts of will, emotion, and reason to solve all difficult problems of life. A balance should be struck between the medieval idea of wholly depending on God and the modern way of sole reliance on the ego.

Use of Will, Feeling, and Reason

As one uses different affirmations, his attitude of mind should change; for example, will affirmations should be accompanied by strong determination; feeling affirmations by devotion; reason affirmations by clear understanding. When healing others, select an affirmation that is suitable to the conative, imaginative, emotional, or thoughtful temperament of your patient. In all affirmations intensity of attention comes first, but continuity and repetition mean a great deal, too. Impregnate your affirmations with devotion, will, and faith, intensely and repeatedly, unmindful of the results, which will come naturally as the fruit of your labours.

During the physical curing process, the attention should not be on the disease, lest one's faith be dampened, but on the infinite powers of the mind. During mental overcoming of fear, anger, bad habits, and so on, one's concentration should be on the opposite quality; that is, the cure for fear is the consciousness of bravery; for anger, peace; for weakness, strength; for sickness, health.

Mental Responsibility for Chronic Diseases

While attempting healing, one often concentrates more on the gripping power of the disease than on the possibility of cure, thus permitting the illness to be a mental as well as a physical habit. This is especially true in most cases of nervousness. Each thought of depression or happiness, irritability or calmness, cuts subtle grooves in the brain cells and strengthens the tendencies toward sickness or well-being.

The subconscious idea-habit of disease or health exerts a strong influence. Stubborn mental or physical diseases always have a deep root in the subconsciousness. Illness may be cured by pulling out its hidden roots. That is why all affirmations of the conscious mind should be *impressive enough* to permeate the subconsciousness, which in turn automatically influences the conscious mind. Strong conscious affirmations thus react on the mind and body through the medium of the subconsciousness. Still stronger affirmations reach not only the subconscious but also the superconscious mind — the magic storehouse of miraculous powers.

Declarations of Truth should be practised willingly, freely, intelligently, and devotionally. One's attention should not be allowed to lag. Straying attention should be brought back again and again like a truant child and repeatedly and patiently trained to perform its given task.

Attention and Faith Are Necessary

All affirmations, in order to reach the superconsciousness, must be free from uncertainties and doubts. Attention and faith are lights that lead even imperfectly understood affirmations to the subconscious and superconscious minds.

Patience and attentive, intelligent repetition are wonder-workers. Affirmations for curing chronic mental or bodily afflictions should be repeated often, deeply and continuously (utterly ignoring unchanged or contrary conditions, if any), until they become part of one's profound intuitional convictions. It is better to die, if death has to come, with the conviction of perfect health than with the thought that a mental or physical ailment is incurable.

Though death may be the necessary end of the body according to present human knowledge, still its "destined hour" may be changed by the power of the soul.

2
Life Energy Causes the Cure

Lord Jesus said: "Man shall not live by bread alone, but by every word that proceedeth out of the mouth of God."*

The "word" is life energy or cosmic vibratory force. The "mouth of God" is the medulla oblongata in the posterior part of the brain, tapering off into the spinal cord. This, the most vital part of the human body, is the divine entrance ("mouth of God") for the "word" or life energy by which man is sustained. In the Hindu

* *Matthew* 4:4. See *John* 1:1(Bible), "In the beginning was the Word, and the Word was with God, and the Word was God."

and Christian scriptures the Word is called, respectively, *Aum* and *Amen*.

It is that Perfect Power alone that heals; all external methods of stimulation only cooperate with the life energy and are valueless without it.

Cure According to Temperament

Medicine, massage, spinal adjustment, or electrical treatment may help to bring back a lost harmonious condition to the cells by chemicalization of the blood or by physiological stimulation. These are external methods that sometimes assist the life energy to effect a cure; but they have no power to act on a dead body, from which the life energy has vanished.

Imagination, reason, faith, emotion, will, or

exertion may be used according to the specific nature of the individual — whether imaginative, intellectual, aspiring, emotional, volitional, or striving. Few people know this. Coué stressed the value of autosuggestion,* but an intellectual type of person is not susceptible to suggestion, and is influenced only by a metaphysical discussion of the power of consciousness over the body. He needs to understand the whys and wherefores of mental power. If he can realize, for instance, that blisters may be produced by hypnosis, as William James points out in *Principles of Psychology,* similarly he can understand the power of the mind to cure disease. If the mind can produce ill health,

* Coué's psychotherapy was based on the power of imagination rather than that of will. He utilized formulas, such as the well-known "Every day, and in every way, I am becoming better and better," which were to be repeated again and again when the mind was in a receptive state, on the theory that they would sink into the subconsciousness and eliminate ideas tending to cause distress and disease.

it can also produce good health. Mind power has developed the different parts of the body; the mind supervises the manufacturing of physical cells and can revitalize them.

Autosuggestion is also powerless to act on the man characterized by strong will power. He can be cured of an ailment by affirmations that stimulate his will rather than his imagination. Autosuggestion, however, is useful to persons whose temperament is chiefly emotional.

The Power of Emotion and Will

A case is recorded of an emotional person who had lost his power of speech, but recovered it as he fled from a burning building. The sudden shock at the sight of flames caused him to shout: "Fire! Fire!"—not remembering that hitherto he had been unable to speak. Strong emotion conquered his subconscious disease-habit. This story illustrates the healing power of intense attention.

During my first steamer trip from India to Ceylon, I was suddenly seized by a spell of seasickness and lost the valuable contents of my stomach. I resented the experience very much; it had been sprung on me at a time when I was enjoying my first experience of a floating room (the cabin) and a swimming village. I determined never again to be tricked like that. I advanced my foot and planted it firmly on the floor of the cabin and commanded my will never again to accept the seasick experience. Later, though I was on the water for a month going to Japan and back to India, and for fifty days from Calcutta to Boston, and for twenty-six days from Seattle to Alaska and back, I was never seasick again.

Stimulation of Life Energy

Will, or imagination, or reason, or emotional powers cannot of themselves effect physical healing. They act only as different agents, which, according to the varying temperaments of individuals, may stimulate the life energy to cure an ailment. In a case of paralysis of the arm, if the will or imagination is continuously stimulated, the life energy may suddenly rush to the diseased nerve tissues and heal the arm.

The repetition of affirmations ought to be firm and continuous, that the strength of the will or reason or emotion be sufficient to stimulate the inactive life energy and to redirect it into normal channels. One should never minimize the importance of *repeated, ever deeper* efforts.

In planting, success depends on two factors:

potency of the seed and suitability of the soil. Similarly, in healing disease, the essentials are the power of the healer and the receptivity of the patient.

"Virtue (that is, healing power) had gone out of him," and "Thy faith hath made thee whole"*: such Biblical sayings show that both the power of the healer and the faith of the sick person are required.

Great healers, men of divine realization, do not cure by chance but by exact knowledge. Fully understanding the control of life energy, they project a stimulating current into the patient that harmonizes his own flow of life energy. During a healing they actually see the psychophysical laws of Nature working in the tissues of the ailing man and bringing about the cure.

* *Mark* 5:30, 34.

Persons of lesser spiritual attainment also are able to heal themselves and others by visualizing and directing an influx of life energy to the affected part of the body.

Instantaneous healing of physical, mental, and spiritual diseases may occur. The accumulated darkness of ages is dispelled at once by bringing the light in, not by trying to chase the darkness out. One cannot tell when he is going to be healed, so do not try to set an exact time limit. Faith, not time, will determine when the cure will be effected. Results depend on the right awakening of life energy and on the conscious and subconscious state of the individual. Disbelief immobilizes the life energy and prevents the perfect working of this divine doctor, body builder, and master mason.

Effort and attention are essential to attain

the degree of faith or will power or imagination that will automatically impel the life energy to effect a cure. Desire for or expectation of results weakens the force of true belief. Without one's use of will and faith, the life energy remains asleep or inoperative.

It takes time to revivify a weakened power of will, faith, or imagination in a patient suffering from a chronic disease, because his brain cells are subtly grooved with thoughts of illness. As it may take a long time to form a bad habit of disease consciousness, similarly some time may be required to form a good habit of health consciousness.

If you affirm, "I am well," but think in the background of your mind that it is not true, the effect is the same as if you took a helpful medicine and at the same time swallowed a drug that counteracted the effects of the medicine. In the use of thought as medicine, you should be careful that you are not neutralizing right thoughts by wrong thoughts. To be active and successful, a thought must be impregnated with such will power that it will resist the opposition of contrary thoughts.

Truth Is the Power in Affirmation

Thoughts have to be understood and applied rightly before they are effective. Ideas first enter man's mind in a crude or undigested form; they need to be assimilated by deep reflection. A thought without soul conviction behind it has no value. That is why persons who use affirmations without comprehending the truth on which they are based—man's inseverable unity with God—get poor results and complain that thoughts have no healing power.

3
Healing Body, Mind, and Soul

In his mortal aspect man is a triune being. He longs for freedom from all varieties of suffering. His needs are:

1. Healing of bodily diseases.

2. Healing of mental or psychological diseases such as fear, anger, bad habits, failure consciousness, lack of initiative and confidence, and so on.

3. Healing of spiritual diseases such as indifference, lack of purpose, intellectual pride and dogmatism, skepticism, contentment with the

material side of existence, and ignorance of the laws of life and of man's own divinity.

It is of paramount importance that equal emphasis be given to the prevention and cure of all three kinds of disease.

The attention of most people is fixed solely on the cure of bodily inharmony, because it is so tangible and obvious. They do not realize that their mental disturbances of worry, egotism, and so on, and their spiritual blindness to the divine meaning of life are the real causes of all human misery.

When a man has destroyed the mental bacteria of intolerance, rage, and fear, and has freed his soul from ignorance, he is unlikely to suffer from physical disease or mental lack.

To Prevent Physical Disease

Obedience to God's physical laws is the method for avoiding bodily ills.

Do not overeat. Most persons die as a result of greediness and of ignorance of right dietary habits.

Obey God's laws of hygiene. The hygiene of keeping the mind pure is superior to physical hygiene, but the latter is important and should not be neglected. Do not, however, live by such rigid rules that the least deviation from your wonted habits upsets you.

Prevent decay in the body by knowledge of the conservation of physical energy and of supplying the body with an inexhaustible amount of life current by Yogoda Satsanga Society exercises.

Prevent hardening of the arteries by proper diet.

Save the heart from overwork; fear and anger overtax it. Give rest to the heart by the Yogoda Satsanga method, and cultivate a peaceful attitude of mind.

Estimating as four ounces the amount of blood expelled by each contraction of the two ventricles of the heart, the weight of the blood output during one minute will amount to eighteen pounds. In a day it will be about twelve tons; in a year, four thousand tons. These figures indicate the enormous amount of labour performed by the heart.

Many persons believe that rest is received by the heart during its diastolic period of expansion, totalling about nine hours out of the twenty-four each day. This period, however, is not true rest; it is only preparation for the systolic movement. The vibrations caused by the contraction of the ventricles reverberate through the tissues of the heart during its relaxation; hence the heart is not at rest.

The energy expended day and night is naturally wearing on the heart muscles. Rest to these muscles would consequently be of great value in maintaining health. Conscious control of sleep, sleeping and waking at will, is part of the yoga training by which man may regulate the beating of the heart. Control over death comes when one can consciously direct the motion of the heart. The rest and renewed energy given to the body by sleep is only a pale reflection of the wonderful calm and strength that come through "conscious sleep," when even the heart rests.

St. Paul said in I *Corinthians* 15:31: "I protest by your rejoicing which I have in Christ Jesus our

Lord, I *die daily*"—that is, the holy peace that comes with Christ Consciousness (*Kutastha Chaitanya*) rests or stops the heart. Many passages in the Bible reveal that the ancient prophets possessed knowledge of the great truth of resting the heart by scientific meditation or by one-pointed devotion to God.

In 1837, in India, a noted *fakir* by the name of Sadhu Haridas was buried underground in a controlled experiment at the order of Maharajah Ranjit Singh of Punjab. The yogi remained buried for forty days inside a walled enclosure under constant military guard. At the end of that time he was exhumed in the presence of many dignitaries of the *durbar* (court), together with Colonel Sir C.M. Wade of London and several other Englishmen from the vicinity. Sadhu Haridas resumed breathing and returned to normal life. In an earlier test conducted by Rajah Dhyan Singh at Jammu, Kashmir, Sadhu Haridas remained buried for four months. He had mastered the art of controlling and resting the heart.

To Prevent Mental Disease

Cultivate peace, and faith in God. Free the mind from all disturbing thoughts and fill it with love and joy. Realize the superiority of mental healing over physical healing. Banish bad habits, which make life miserable.

To Prevent Spiritual Disease

Spiritualize the body by destruction of the consciousness of mortality and change. The body is materialized vibration and should be cognized as such. The consciousness of disease, decay, and death should be removed by scientific understanding of the underlying unifying laws of matter and Spirit, and of the delusive manifestation of Spirit as matter, of the Infinite as finite. Firmly believe that you are created in the image of the Father and are therefore immortal and perfect.

Even a particle of matter or a wave of energy is indestructible, as science has proved; the soul or spiritual essence of man is also indestructible. Matter undergoes change; the soul undergoes changing experiences. Radical changes are termed death, but death or a change in form does not change or destroy the spiritual essence.

Various methods of concentration and meditation are taught, but the Yogoda Satsanga methods are the most effective. Apply in your daily life the experiences of peace and poise you receive during concentration and meditation. Maintain your equilibrium amidst trying circumstances. Do not abandon yourself to violent emotions; stand unshaken by adverse turns of events.

Evaluation of Curative Methods

Disease is generally considered a result of external material causes. Few people realize that it comes through the inaction of the life force within. When the cell or tissue vehicle of the life energy is seriously damaged, the life energy withdraws from that place and trouble consequently starts. Medicine, massage, and electricity merely help to stimulate the cells in such a way that the life energy is induced to return and resume its work of maintenance and repair.

We should not be extremists in any way

but should adopt whatever methods of healing are suitable, according to individual conviction. Medicines and food have a definite chemical action upon blood and tissues. So long as one eats food, why should one deny that medicines and other material aids also have an effect on the body? They are useful so long as the material consciousness in man is uppermost. They have their limitations, however, because they are applied from outside. The best methods are those that help the life energy to resume its internal healing activities.

Medicine may chemically help the blood and tissues. Use of electrical devices may also be beneficial. But neither medicine nor electricity can cure disease; they can only stimulate or coax the life energy back to the neglected diseased body part. The introduction of a foreign element, be it medicine or electricity or any other intermediary aid, is undesirable if we can manage to use the life force directly.

God's Laws as Applied to Matter

Salves may be useful for itches, sores, cuts, and so on. If your arm or leg has been fractured, it is unnecessary to give the life energy the trouble of joining the displaced bones when a surgeon (a child of God and hence capable of serving as His instrument) can set them by use of his skill and knowledge of God's laws as applied to matter. If you can instantaneously heal your broken bones by mental power, do so; but it would be unwise to wait until you have attained that power.

By fasting, massage, osteopathic treatment,

chiropractic adjustment of the vertebrae, yoga postures, and so on, we may help to remove or relieve congestion in the nerves or vertebrae and permit the free flow of life energy.

Acquiring Power Over Life Energy

On the other hand, mental cure is superior to all methods of physical cure because will, imagination, faith, and reason are states of consciousness that actually and directly act from within. They furnish the motive power that stimulates and directs the life energy to accomplish any definite task.

Autosuggestion and various affirmations are useful in stimulating the life energy; but because a practitioner often employs such purely mental methods without consciously working with the life energy, thus failing to establish any physiological connection, they are not invariably efficacious. A cure is certain if psychophysical techniques are combined with the power of will, faith, and reason to direct the life energy and to reach the superconscious mind. In that blissful state of Reality one comprehends the inseparable unity of matter and Spirit and solves all problems of inharmony.

Yogoda Satsanga teachings give the *modus operandi* for harnessing the will to direct the movement of actually vibrating life energy to any body part. By this method one feels in a definite way the inner flow of cosmic vibratory force.

4
The Nature of Creation

Matter does not exist in the way we usually conceive it; nevertheless, it does exist as a cosmic delusion. To dispel delusion requires a definite method. You cannot cure a drug addict in a moment. Material consciousness possesses man through a law of delusion, and he cannot banish it except by learning and following the opposite law, that of truth.

Spirit, through a series of processes of materialization, became matter; hence matter proceeds from and cannot be different from its cause, Spirit. Matter is a partial expression of Spirit, the

Infinite appearing as finite, the Unlimited as limited. But since matter is only Spirit in a delusive manifestation, matter per se is nonexistent.

Consciousness and Matter

At the start of creation, the hitherto unmanifested Spirit projected two natures—one, consciousness, and the other, matter. They are Its two vibratory expressions. Consciousness is a finer, and matter a grosser, vibration of the one transcendental Spirit.

Consciousness is the vibration of Its subjective aspect, and matter is the vibration of Its objective aspect. Spirit, as Cosmic Consciousness, is potentially immanent in objective vibratory matter, and manifests Itself subjectively as the consciousness present in all forms of creation, reaching Its highest expression in the human mind with its countless ramifications of thoughts, feelings, will, and imagination.

The difference between matter and Spirit is in the rate of vibration — a difference of degree, not of kind. This point may be better understood by the following example. Although all vibrations are qualitatively alike, vibrations from 16 to 20,000 cycles per second are gross enough to be audible to man's sense of hearing, but vibrations below 16 or over 20,000 are generally inaudible. There is no essential difference between audible and inaudible vibrations, though a relative difference does exist.

Through the power of *maya,* cosmic illusion, the Creator has caused the manifestations of matter to appear so distinct and specific that to the human mind they seem unrelated in any way to Spirit.

Thought Is the Subtlest Vibration

Within the gross vibration of flesh is the fine vibration of the cosmic current, the life energy; and permeating both flesh and life energy is the most subtle vibration, that of consciousness.

The vibrations of consciousness are so subtle that they cannot be detected by any material instrument; only consciousness can comprehend consciousness. Human beings are aware of the myriad vibrations of consciousness issuing from other human beings—expressed by word, act, look, gesture, silence, attitude, and so on.

Each man is stamped with the vibratory signature of his own state of consciousness, and emanates a characteristic influence on persons and things. For example, a room in which a man lives is permeated with his thought vibrations.

These may be distinctly felt by other persons if they possess the required degree of sensitivity.

Man's ego (his sense of I-ness; the distorted mortal reflection of the immortal soul) cognizes consciousness directly; and congnizes matter (the human body and all other objects in creation) indirectly, through mental processes and through sense perceptions. That is, the ego is always aware of possessing consciousness; but the ego is not aware of matter, even of the body it inhabits, until it takes thought about it. Thus a man in deep concentration on any subject is conscious of his mind but not of his body.

Man's Experiences in the Dream State

All the experiences of man's waking state can be duplicated in his dream state of consciousness. In the dream state a man may find himself walking joyously in a lovely garden and then seeing the dead body of a friend. He is grief-stricken, sheds tears, suffers from headache, and feels his heart throb painfully. Perhaps a rainstorm blows up suddenly and he becomes wet and cold. Then he wakes up and laughs at his illusory dream experiences.

What is the difference between the experiences of a dreaming man (experience of *matter* as displayed in the bodies of himself and his friend, the garden, and so on; and experiences of *consciousness* as displayed in his feelings of joy and grief) and the experiences of the same man in the waking state? Awareness of matter and of consciousness is present in both cases.

Man is able to create both matter and consciousness in an illusory dream world; therefore it should not be difficult for him to realize that Spirit, utilizing the power of *maya,* has created for man a dream world of "life" or conscious existence that in essence is as false (because ephemeral, ever changing) as are man's experiences in the dream state.

Maya or Cosmic Illusion

The phenomenal world operates under *maya,* the law of duality or oppositional states; it is thus an unreal world that veils the truth of the Divine Oneness and Unchangeableness. Man in his mortal aspect dreams of dualities and contrasts — life and death, health and disease, happiness and sorrow; but when he awakens in soul consciousness all dualities disappear and he knows himself as the eternal and blissful Spirit.

The Needs of Erring Humanity

For erring humanity both medical and mental help are important. The superiority of the mind over material aids is undeniable, but the more limited healing power of food and herbs and drugs is also undeniable. When employing mental methods, there is no need to scorn all physical systems of cure, for the latter are the outcome of investigation into God's material laws.

So long as one's material consciousness of the body exists, medicines need not be entirely dispensed with; but as soon as man increases his understanding of the immaterial origin of flesh, his belief in the healing power of drugs disappears: he sees that all disease has its roots in the mind.

"Wisdom Is the Greatest Cleanser"

My master, Swami Sri Yukteswarji, never spoke of the uselessness of drugs; yet he so trained and expanded the consciousness of many of his students that they used only mental power to cure themselves when ill. He often said: "Wisdom is the greatest cleanser."

Some persons, in both East and West, fanatically deny the existence of matter while they are still so engrossed in flesh consciousness that they feel famished if they miss a meal.

The state of realization in which body and mind, death and life, disease and health all appear *equally delusive* is the only state in which we can truly say that we do not believe in the existence of matter.

Human and Divine Consciousness

Through *maya* and man's consequent ignorance of his soul, human consciousness is isolated from Cosmic Consciousness. The mind of man is subject to change and limitation, but Cosmic Consciousness is free from all restrictions and is never involved in experiences of duality (death and life, disease and health, fleeting sorrow and fleeting joy, and so on). In the Divine Mind an unchangeable perception of Bliss is ever present.

The process of liberating human consciousness consists in training it by study, affirmations, concentration, and meditation to turn its attention away from the vibrations of the gross body with its ceaseless fluctuations of thought and emotion, and to feel the subtler and more stable vibrations of life energy and of higher mental states.

Rely on the Divine Power Within

Persons whose material consciousness is strong, i.e., those accustomed to thinking of the "self" as the physical body, need to be gradually guided away from dependence on medicine and other outer aids and taught to rely more and more on the Divine Power within.

PART II

METHOD OF PRACTICE

5
Technique of Affirmation

Preliminary Rules

1. Sit facing north or east on a wool blanket in Padmasana (the Lotus Pose) or in any easy cross-legged pose, or on a straight armless chair over which a wool blanket has been placed. The cloth serves as an insulation against magnetic earth currents that tend to tie the mind to material perceptions

2. Close your eyes and concentrate on the medulla oblongata (at the back of the neck), unless otherwise directed. Keep spine erect, chest

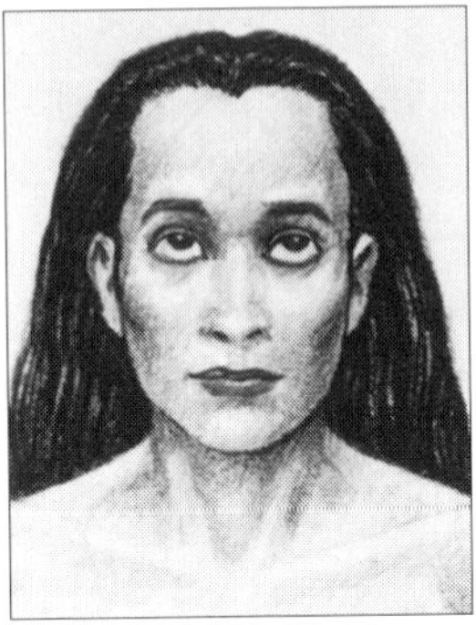

SRI SRI MAHAVATAR BABAJI
Guru of Sri Sri Lahiri Mahasaya

SRI SRI LAHIRI MAHASAYA
(Shyama Charan Lahiri)
Guru of Sri Sri Swami
Sri Yukteswar Giri

SRI SRI SWAMI
SRI YUKTESWAR GIRI
Guru of Sri Sri
Paramahansa Yogananda

DIRECT DISCIPLES OF YOGANANDAJI WHO SUCCEEDED HIM AS SPIRITUAL HEAD OF YSS/SRF

(*Left to right*) Sri Rajarsi Janakananda, spiritual head and president of Yogoda Satsanga Society of India/Self-Realization Fellowship 1952–1955. Sri Daya Mata succeeded Rajarsi Janakananda in February 1955, serving in these roles for more than 55 years until her passing in 2010. Sri Mrinalini Mata, another close disciple of the great master chosen and trained by him as one of those to lead his work after his passing, fulfilled these responsibilities from early 2011 until her passing in 2017. Sri Swami Chidananda Giri, a YSS/SRF monastic for over 40 years, is the current president and spiritual head of YSS/SRF. For more information on the YSS/SRF lineage please visit our website, www.yssofindia.org.

high, abdomen in. Take a deep breath and exhale it, three times.

3. Relax the body and keep it motionless. Empty the mind of all restless thoughts, and withdraw its attention from bodily sensations, heat and cold, sounds, and so on.

4. Do not think of the particular kind of healing you need.

5. Cast away anxiety, distrust, and worry. Realize calmly and trustingly that the Divine Law works and is all-powerful. Permit yourself no doubt or disbelief. Faith and concentration allow the law to operate unhampered. Hold the thought that all bodily states are changeable and curable and that the idea of a chronic disease is a delusion.

Time: One should use affirmations immediately after awakening in the morning or during the period of somnolence preceding sleep at night. Groups may meet at any suitable hour.

Place: Quiet surroundings as far as possible. If the meeting has to be held in a noisy place, ignore the sounds and attend devotedly to your practice.

Method: Before starting to affirm, always free the mind from worries and restlessness. Choose your affirmation and repeat all of it, first loudly, then softly and more slowly, until your voice becomes a whisper. Then gradually affirm it mentally only, without moving the tongue or the lips, until you feel that you have attained deep, unbroken concentration—not unconsciousness, but a profound continuity of uninterrupted thought.

If you continue with your mental affirmation, and go still deeper, you will feel a sense of increasing joy and peace. During the state of deep concentration, your affirmation will merge with the subconscious stream, to come back later reinforced with power to influence your conscious mind through the law of habit.

During the time that you experience ever increasing peace, your affirmation goes deeper, into the superconscious realm, to return later laden with unlimited power to influence your conscious mind and also to fulfil your desires. Doubt not and you shall witness the miracle of this scientific faith.

During group affirmations for curing physical and mental disease in yourself or others, the group should take care to affirm with an even tone, even mental force, even concentration, and even sense of faith and peace.

Weaker minds lessen the united force born of affirmations and may even sidetrack this flood of power from its superconscious destination. Therefore one should not make bodily movements or become mentally restless. The concentration of all members of the group is necessary for success.

In group affirmations the leader should read the affirmations rhythmically. Then the audience should repeat the same words with the same rhythm and intonation.

THESE AFFIRMATIONS SOUL-INSPIRED

The affirmation seeds in this book have been impregnated with soul inspiration. They should be sown in the soil of superconscious peace and watered by your faith and concentration to create inner motile vibrations that will help the seeds to germinate.

Many processes are involved between the sowing of the affirmation seed and its fruition.

All conditions of its growth must be fulfilled to produce the desired result. The affirmation seed must be a living one, free from the defects of doubt, restlessness, or inattention; it should be sown in the mind and heart with concentration, devotion, and peace, and watered with deep, fresh repetition and boundless faith.

Always avoid mechanical repetition. This meaning is found in the Biblical injunction: "Thou shalt not take the name of the Lord thy God in vain."* Repeat affirmations firmly and with intensity and sincerity until such power is gained that one command, one strong urge from within, will be sufficient to change your body cells and to move your soul to performance of miracles.

* Exodus 20:7.

The Progressive Stages of Chanting

Remember again that the affirmations should be uttered with the proper loud intonation, fading into a whisper, and above all with attention and devotion. Thus the thoughts are led, by one's conviction of the efficacy and truth of the affirmations, from the auditory sense to the understanding of the conscious mind, then to the subconscious or automatic mind, and then to the superconscious mind. Those persons who believe will be cured by these affirmations.

The five stages of chanting are: conscious loud chanting, whisper chanting, mental chanting, subconscious chanting, and superconscious chanting.

Aum or Amen, the Cosmic Sound

Subconscious chanting becomes unbroken and automatic. Superconscious chanting results when the deep internal chanting vibrations are converted into realization and are established in the conscious, subconscious, and superconscious minds. Holding the attention uninterruptedly on the true Cosmic Vibration (*Aum* or Amen), not on an imaginary sound, is superconscious chanting.

When you are passing from one stage of chanting to another, the attitude of the mind also should change and become deeper and more concentrated. The aim is to unite chanter, chant, and the process of chanting into one. The mind should enter the deepest conscious state—not unconsciousness or absentmindedness or sleep, but a state of such focused concentration that all thoughts are sunk into and merged with the one central thought, like particles drawn to an irresistible magnet.

Three Physiological Centres

During will affirmations, your attention should be centred in the spot between the eyebrows; during thought affirmations, in the medulla oblongata;* and during devotional affirmations, in the heart. At appropriate times

* The medulla and the spot between the eyebrows are in fact the negative and positive poles, respectively, of one center of intelligent life force. Paramahansaji sometimes instructed devotees to concentrate at the spot between the eyebrows, and sometimes at the medulla, but the two are one by polarity. When the gaze of the eyes is centralized with calm concentration at the point between the eyebrows, the current from the two eyes goes first to that point in the forehead, and thence to the medulla. The single astral eye of light then appears in the forehead, reflected there from the medulla.

man automatically fixes his mind on one of these physiological regions; for example, during states of emotion he feels the heart centre to the exclusion of all other parts of the body. By the practice of affirmations one acquires the power of consciously directing his attention to the vital sources of will, thought, and feeling.

Absolute, unquestioning faith in God is the greatest method of instantaneous healing. An unceasing effort to arouse that faith is man's highest and most rewarding duty.

6
Scientific Healing Affirmations

In using the affirmations in this book, the individual devotee or the group leader may read uninterruptedly through an entire affirmation or may stop and repeat whatever lines he wishes.

Affirmations for General Healing

On every altar of feeling,
Thought, and will,
Thou art sitting,

Thou art sitting.
Thou art all feeling, will, and thought.
Thou dost guide them;
Let them follow, let them follow,
Let them be as Thou art.

In the temple of consciousness
There was the light—Thy light.
I saw it not; now I see,
The temple is light, the temple is whole.
I slept and dreamt that the temple broke
With fear, worry, ignorance.
I slept and dreamt that the temple broke
With fear, worry, ignorance.
Thou hast wakened me,
Thou hast wakened me.
Thy temple is whole,
Thy temple is whole.

I want to worship Thee,
I want to worship Thee.
In the heart, in the star,
In the body cell I love Thee;
In the electron I play with Thee.
I wish to worship Thee
In body, star, stardust, nebula.
Thou art everywhere; everywhere
I worship Thee.

Celestial will of Thine
As human will of mine
Doth shine, doth shine
In me, in me, in me, in me.
I will wish, I will will,
I will work, I will drill,
Not led by ego, but by Thee,
But by Thee, but by Thee.

I will work, exert my will;
But charge my will
With Thine own will, with Thine own will.

Make us little children, O Father,
Even as Thy kingdom contains such.
Thy love in us is perfection.
Even as Thou art whole, so are we whole.
In body and mind we are healthy,
Even as Thou art, even as Thou art.
Thou art perfect.
We are Thy children.

Thou art everywhere;
Where'er Thou art, perfection's there.
Thou art sitting in every altar cell,
Thou art in all my body cells.
They are whole; they are perfect.

They are whole; they are perfect.
Make me feel Thou art there
In them all, in them all;
Make me feel Thou art there
In each and all, in each and all.

Life of my life, Thou art whole.
Thou art everywhere;
In my heart, in my brain,
In my eyes, in my face,
In my limbs and all.

Thou dost move my feet;
They are whole, they are whole.
My calves and thighs
Are whole, are whole, for Thou art there.
My thighs are held by Thee
Lest I fall, lest I fall.

They are whole, for Thou art there.
They are whole, for Thou art there.

Thou art in my throat;
Mucous membrane, abdomen,
Glisten with Thee.
They are whole, for Thou art there.
In my spine Thou dost sparkle;
It is whole, it is whole.
In my nerves Thou dost flow;
They are whole, they are whole.
In my veins and arteries
Thou dost float, Thou dost float.
They are whole, they are whole.
Thou art fire in my stomach;
Thou art fire in my intestines;
They are whole, they are whole.

Even as Thou art mine own
So am I Thine own.
Thou art perfect;
Thou art I, Thou art I.
Thou art my brain;
It is shining, it is whole,
It is whole, it is whole, it is whole.

Let my fancy flow free;
Let my fancy flow free.
I am ill when so I think;
I am well when so I think;
Every hour, oh, every day
In body, mind, in every way
I am whole, I am well.
I am whole, I am well.

I dreamt a dream that I was ill;
I woke and laughed to find me still
Bedewed with tears,
But tears of joy, not sadness;
To find I had dreamt of sickness;
For I am whole, I am whole.

Let me feel
Thy loving thrill, Thy loving thrill.
Thou art my Father,
I am Thy child.
Good or naughty,
I am Thy child.
Let me feel Thy healthy thrill;
Let me feel Thy wisdom's will.
Let me feel Thy wisdom's will.

Brief Affirmations

Perfect Father, Thy light is flowing through Bhagavan Krishna, Jesus Christ, through the saints of all religions, through the masters of India, and through me. This divine light is present in all my body parts. I am well.

O Conscious Cosmic Energy, Thy life is mine. Solid, liquid, and gaseous foods are converted and spiritualized into energy by Thee to support my body.

I am renewed and strengthened by Thy life-giving energy.

The healing power of Spirit is flowing through all the cells of my body. I am made of the one universal God-substance.

Father, Thou art in me; I am well.

Thy power is moving through me. My stomach is well, for Thy healing light is there.

I recognize my illness to be the result of my transgression against health laws. I will undo the evil by right eating, exercise, and right thinking.

Heavenly Father, Thou art present in every atom, every cell, every corpuscle, every particle of nerve, brain and tissue. I am well, for Thou art in all my body parts.

God's perfect health permeates the dark nooks of my bodily sickness. In all my cells His healing light is shining. They are entirely well, for His perfection is in them.

Affirmation by Power of Thought

Concentrate your thought on the forehead, and repeat the following:

I think my life to flow,
I know my life to flow,
From brain to all my body to flow.
Streaks of light do shoot
Through my tissue root.
The flood of life in vertebrae
Doth rush through spine in froth and spray;
The little cells all are drinking;
Their tiny mouths all are shining;
The little cells all are drinking;
Their tiny mouths all are shining.

Brief Affirmations

Heavenly Father, Thou art mine forever. In everything that is good I worship Thy presence. Through the windows of all pure thoughts I behold Thy goodness.

O Father, Thine unlimited and all-healing power is in me. Manifest Thy light through the darkness of my ignorance. Wherever this healing light is present, there is perfection. Therefore, perfection is in me.

Heavenly Father, Thou art all feeling, will, and thought. Guide Thou my feeling, will, and thought; let them follow, let them be as Thou art.

My dreams of perfection are the bridges that carry me into the realm of pure ideas.

Daily I will seek happiness more and more within my mind, and less and less through material pleasures.

God is the shepherd of my restless thoughts. He will lead them to His abode of peace.

I will purify my mind with the thought that God is guiding my every activity.

The Right Guidance of Reason

Follow the suggestions outlined below to stimulate right reasoning and mental activity.

1. Read good books and carefully digest their message.

2. If you read one hour, then write for two hours, and reflect for three hours. This is the proportion that should be observed to cultivate the power of reason.

3. Occupy your mind with inspiring ideas. Do not waste time in negative thinking.

4. Adopt the best plan for your life that you can formulate by the exercise of reason.

5. Strengthen your reasoning powers by studying the laws of the mind, outlined in the teachings of Yogoda Satsanga Society.

6. Use the affirmations in this book, uttered with soul force, to develop the power of your mind. Ancient and modern psychologists have pointed out that the innate intelligence of man

is capable of infinite expansion.

7. Obey physical, social, and moral laws. By believing them to be controlled by a superior spiritual law, you will eventually rise above all lesser laws and be guided wholly by spiritual law.

Affirmation by Power of Will

Concentrate your will simultaneously on the medulla oblongata and on the spot between the eyebrows, and repeat the following—first loudly and gradually more softly, until you are whispering:

I will life-force to charge—
With Godly will I will it charge—
Through my nerves and muscles all,
My tissues, limbs, and all,

With vibrant tingling fire,
With burning joyous power.
In blood and glands,
By sovereign command,
I bid you flow.
By my command
I bid you glow.
By my command
I bid you glow.

Affirmations for Wisdom

Concentrate on the region beneath the top of the skull, feeling there the presence of the brain.

In wisdom's chambers
Thou dost roam.

Thou art the reason in me.
Oh, Thou dost roam and wake
Each lazy little cell of brain
To receive, to receive
The good that mind and senses give,
The knowledge that Thou dost give.

I will think, I will reason;
I won't trouble Thee for thought;
But lead Thou me when reason errs;
To its goal lead it right.

O Heavenly Father, O Cosmic Mother,
O Master Mine, O Friend Divine,
I came alone, I go alone;
With Thee alone, with Thee alone.
With Thee alone, with Thee alone.

Oh, Thou didst make a home for me
Of living cells, a home for me.
This home of mine is home of Thine;
Thy life did make this home;
Thy strength did make this home.
Thy home is perfect, Thy home is perfect.

I am Thy child, Thou art my Father;
We both do dwell, we both do dwell
In temple same,
In this temple of cells,
Oh, in this temple of cells.
Thou art always here,
Oh, on my throbbing altar near.

I went away, I went away;
With darkness to play, with error to play;
A truant child, I went away.

Home I came in shadows dark,
Home I came with matter's muddy mark.
Thou art near; I cannot see.
Thy home is perfect; I cannot see.
I am blind; Thy light is there.
'Tis my fault that I cannot see.
Oh, 'tis my fault that I cannot see.
Beneath the darkness line
  Thy light doth shine;
  Thy light doth shine.

Together, light and darkness
Cannot stay, cannot stay.
Together, wisdom, ignorance,
Cannot stay, cannot stay.
Conjure away, oh, lure away,
  The darkness away,
  My darkness away.

My body cells are made of light,
My fleshly cells are made of Thee.
They are perfect, for Thou art perfect;
They are healthy, for Thou art Health;
They are Spirit, for Thou art Spirit;
They are immortal, for Thou art Life.

Brief Affirmations

Heavenly Father, Thy cosmic life and I are one. Thou art the ocean, I am the wave; we are one.

I demand my divine birthright, intuitively Realizing that all wisdom and power already exist in my soul.

God is just behind my reason, today and

every day, and is guiding me to do the right thing always.

God is the indwelling Self of man and the sole Life of the whole universe.

I am submerged in eternal light. It permeates every particle of my being. I am living in that light. The Divine Spirit fills me within and without.

God is within and around me, protecting me; so I will banish the fear that shuts out His guiding light.

Perfect peace and poise are mine today, as I concentrate all my power and ability upon expressing the divine will.

The Subconscious, Conscious, and Superconscious Laws for Material Success

Success comes by obeying the divine and the material laws. Both material and spiritual success should be attained. Material success consists in possessing the necessities of life.

Ambition for money-making should include a desire to help others. Acquire all the money you can by improving in some way your community or country or the world, but never seek financial gain by acting against their interests.

There are subconscious, conscious, and superconscious laws for material success and for overcoming a failure-attitude of mind.

The subconscious law of success is to repeat

affirmations intensely and attentively immediately before sleep and after sleep. Doubt not; when you want to attain any righteous goal, cast away the thought of failure. As you are a child of God, believe that you have access to all things that belong to Him.

Ignorance of and disbelief in this law have deprived man of his immortal heritage. To utilize the resources of divine supply, you should destroy the subconscious seeds of erroneous thoughts by steady repetition of affirmations saturated with infinite confidence.

The conscious law of success is to plan and act intelligently, feeling at all times that God is helping you in your planning and your ceaseless hard work.

The superconscious law of success is put into operation through man's prayers and by his understanding of the Lord's omnipotence. Do not stop your conscious efforts or rely wholly on your own natural abilities, but ask divine aid in all you do.

When these subconscious, conscious, and superconscious methods are combined, success is certain. Try again, no matter how many times you have failed.

Affirmation for Material Success

Thou art my Father:
Success and joy.
I am Thy child:
Success and joy.

All the wealth of this earth,

All the riches of the universe,
Belong to Thee, belong to Thee.
I am Thy child;
The wealth of earth and universe
Belongs to me, belongs to me,
Oh, belongs to me, belongs to me.

I lived in thoughts of poverty
And wrongly fancied I was poor,
So I was poor.
Now I am home. Thy consciousness
Hath made me wealthy, made me rich.
I am successful, I am rich;
Thou art my Treasure,
I am rich, I am rich.

Thou art everything, Thou art everything.
Thou art mine.

I have everything, I have everything;
I am wealthy, I am rich.
I have everything, I have everything;
I possess all and everything,
Even as Thou dost, even as Thou dost.
I possess everything, I possess everything.
Thou art my Wealth,
I have everything.

Brief Affirmations

I know that God's power is limitless; and as I am made in His image, I, too, have the strength to overcome all obstacles.

I possess the creative power of Spirit. The Infinite Intelligence will guide me and solve every problem.

God is my own inexhaustible Divine Bank. I am always rich, for I have access to the Cosmic Storehousee.

I will go forth in perfect faith in the power of Omnipresent Good to bring me what I need at the time I need it.

The sunshine of divine prosperity has just burst through the dark sky of my limitations. I am God's child. What He has, I have.

Banishing Soul Ignorance

Spiritual success lies in consciously attuning yourself with the Cosmic Mind, and in maintaining your peace and poise no matter what irremediable events occur in your life, such as the death of relatives or other losses. When you are separated from one of your dear ones by the law of Nature, you should not sorrow. Instead, thank God humbly that for a time He gave you the privilege of tending and befriending and keeping in your charge one of His children.

Spiritual success comes by understanding the mystery of life; and by looking on all things cheerfully and courageously, Realizing that events proceed according to a beautiful divine plan.

For the disease of ignorance, the only cure is knowledge.

Affirmations for Spiritual Success

Thou art Wisdom,
And Thou dost know

The cause and end of all things.
I am Thy child;
I want to know
Life's true mystery,
Life's true joyous duty.

Thy wisdom in me shall show
All things that Thou dost know,
That Thou dost know.

Brief Affirmations

Heavenly Father, my voice was made to sing Thy glory. My heart was made to respond to Thy call alone. My soul was made to be a channel through which Thy love might flow uninterruptedly into all thirsty souls.

The power of Thy love crucifies all my

thoughts of doubt and fear, that I may rise triumphant over death and ascend on wings of light to Thee.

I relax and cast aside all mental burdens, allowing God to express through me His perfect love, peace, and wisdom.

My Heavenly Father is love, and I am made in His image. I am the sphere of love in which all planets, all stars, all beings, all creation are glimmering. I am the love that pervades the whole universe.

As I radiate love and goodwill to others, I will open the channel for God's love to come to me. Divine love is the magnet that draws to me all good.

I can perform all duties only after borrowing the powers of action from God, so my first desire is to please Him. The first love of my heart, the first ambition of my soul, the first goal of my will and reason is God alone.

Affirmation for Psychological Success

I am brave, I am strong.
Perfume of success thoughts
Blows in me, blows in me.
I am cool, I am calm,
I am sweet, I am kind,
I am love and sympathy,
I am charming and magnetic,
I am pleased with all;
I wipe away all tears and fears.
I have no enemy.
I am the friend of all.

I have no habits,
In eating, thinking, behaving;
I am free, I am free.

I command Thee, O Attention,
To come and practice concentration
On things I do, on works I do.
I can do everything
When so I think, when so I think.

In church or temple, in prayer mood,
My vagrant thoughts against me stood,
And held my mind from reaching Thee,
And held my mind from reaching Thee.
Teach me to own again, oh, own again,
My matter-sold mind and brain,
That I may give them to Thee
In prayer and ecstasy,
In meditation and reverie.

I will worship Thee
In meditation and seclusion.
I will feel Thine energy
Flowing through my hands in activity.
Lest in sloth I lose Thee,
I will find Thee in activity.

Combined Methods

While the superiority of mental, rather than material, methods of cure is undeniable, a few physical exercises are included in this book for those who desire to combine both methods.

Improving the Eyesight

Concentrate with closed eyes on the medulla oblongata, then feel the power of vision in the eyes flowing through the optic nerve into the retina. After concentrating for a minute on the retina, open and close your eyes a few times. Turn the eyeballs upward, then downward; then to the left, then to the right. Then move them from left to right, and right to left. Fix your gaze on the spot between the eyebrows, visualizing the flow of life energy from the medulla oblongata into the eyes, transforming them into two searchlights. This exercise is beneficial physically and mentally.

Affirmation for the Eyes

I bid you,
O rays of blue,
To glide through my optic nerves
And show me true, and show me true
His light is there,
His light is there.
Through my eyes
He doth peep,
He doth peep;
They are whole, they are perfect.
One* above and two below;
Eyes three, eyes three.
Through you, unseen, what light doth flee,
Through you, unseen, what light doth flee!

* The "single" or spiritual eye in the forehead between the two eyebrows. See footnote on page 59.

Lotus eyes, weep no more,
Weep no more.
The storms thy petals hurt no more.
Come quick and glide like swans,
In the blithesome waters of bliss,
In the gentle lake of peace,
In the hour of wisdom's dawn.
This light of Thine,
Oh, shines through mine,
Through past, present, and future time.

I command you,
My eyes two,
Be one and single,
Be one and single.
To see all and know all;
To make my body shine,
To make my mind shine,
To make my soul shine.

Exercise for the Stomach

Standing in front of a chair, bend forward and grasp the seat for support. Exhale the breath completely. While the breath is expelled, draw in the abdomen as near the backbone as possible. Then inhale while you push out the abdomen as far as possible. Repeat twelve times. Yogis state that this exercise improves the functioning of the digestive tract (the peristaltic action of the intestines, and the secretions of the digestive glands), and thereby aids in removing stomach ailments.

Exercise for the Teeth

With your eyes closed, clench the upper and lower teeth on the left side of your jaw. Relax, then clench the teeth on the right side. Relax, then clench the front teeth. Finally, clench all the upper and lower teeth simultaneously.

Hold each position for one or two minutes, concentrating on the "clenched-teeth" sensation and visualizing the life energy as vitalizing the roots of the teeth and removing all inharmonious conditions.

The Eden Within

The body is a garden that contains the charming trees of the senses—sight, sound, taste, smell, and touch. God or the Divinity in man warns him against immoderation in the use of any of the sense fruits; and especially against the wrong use of the apple of sex force, situated in the midst of the bodily garden.

The serpent of evil curiosity and the Eve or emotional feminine nature present in all human beings tempt them to disobey God's command. Thus they lose the joy of self-control and are driven from the Eden of purity and divine bliss. Sex experience brings in the sin or "fig leaf" consciousness of shame.

Married couples who desire children should confine their attention during the act of mating to its creative purpose. To avoid many sufferings, humanity should not seek sex communion for its own sake.

Methods for Sex Control

Before retiring at night, wipe with a cold, wet towel all body openings as well as the hands, feet, armpits, navel, and the back of the neck over the medulla oblongata. Do this regularly.

During times of bodily excitement draw six to fifteen deep breaths and exhale them deeply. Then quickly seek the company of those you respect, persons of self-control.

Affirmations for Purity

Through stamen and pistil
Thou dost create the flowers pure.
Through my parents pure
My body Thou didst bring.
Even as Thou art the Creator
Of all good things,
So are we.
Teach us to create
In sacredness, in holiness,
Noble ideas or noble children.

Thou art sexless.
We are sexless, we are sexless.
Thou didst create us in purity.

Teach us to create in sacredness
Noble thoughts or children
Wrought in Thine image.

To conquer temptations I will drive evil from my thoughts. I will withdraw my mind from sense regions on the outer surface of the body, which give rise to mental longings, and will seek the inner bliss of God's presence.

Curing Bad Habits

Good habits are your best helpers; preserve their power by continual good actions.

Bad habits are your worst enemies; against your will they force on you an injurious course of conduct. They are detrimental to your physical, social, moral, mental, and spiritual life. Starve wrong habits by refusing them the food of further bad actions.

True freedom lies in performing all actions in accordance with right judgement and free choice. For example, eat what you know you should eat, not necessarily what you have become used to.

Good and bad habits both take time to acquire real power. Long-continued bad habits can be displaced by good habits if the latter are patiently cultivated.

Crowd out bad habits by substituting good habits in all departments of your life. Strengthen the consciousness of your freedom, as a child of God, from all inner compulsions.

Affirmation for Freedom

Thou art in law;
Thou art above all laws,
Thou art above all laws.
Even as Thou art,
Above all laws am I.

O ye brave good soldier habits
Drive away the dark, dark habits;
Drive away the dark, dark habits.
I am free, I am free.
I have no habits, I have no habits.
I'll do what's right, I'll do what's right,
Uncommanded by habits' might.
I am free, I am free;
I have no habits, I have no habits.

Brief Affirmations

Heavenly Father, strengthen my determination to discard wrong habits, which attract evil vibrations, and to form right habits, which attract good vibrations.

The eternal life of God flows through me. I am immortal. Behind the wave of my mind is the ocean of Cosmic Consciousness.

Divine Father, where Thou has placed me, there Thou must come.

No moving picture of life is made up of only one player or one event. My part on the stage is important, for without me the cosmic drama would be incomplete.

Prayers to the Divine Father

Prayers should be used, not to beg for transitory favours, but to enable man to reclaim the divine treasure that in his ignorance he had thought lost. The following prayers will turn your thoughts to God — the Source of all good and the Power in all affirmations.

Since Thine indelible image of perfection is in me, teach me to wipe away the superficial stains of ignorance and see that Thou and I are One.

O Spirit, teach me to heal the body by recharging it with Thy cosmic energy, to heal the mind by concentration and cheerfulness, and the soul by meditation-born intuition. Let Thy kingdom that is within manifest itself without.

Heavenly Father, teach me to remember Thee in poverty or prosperity, in sickness or health, in ignorance or wisdom. May I open my closed eyes of unbelief and behold Thine instantaneously healing light.

Divine Shepherd, rescue the lambkins of my thoughts, lost in the wilderness of restlessness, and lead them into Thy sacred fold of peace.

Beloved God, may I know that Thine unseen, all-protecting mantle is ever around me, in joy and in sorrow, in life and in death.

About the Author

"The ideal of love for God and service to humanity found full expression in the life of Paramahansa Yogananda.... Though the major part of his life was spent outside India, still he takes his place among our great saints. His work continues to grow and shine ever more brightly, drawing people everywhere on the path of the pilgrimage of the Spirit."

In these words, the Government of India paid tribute to the founder of Yogoda Satsanga Society of India/Self-Realization Fellowship, upon issuing a commemorative stamp in his honour on March 7, 1977, the twenty-fifth anniversary of his passing.

A world teacher whose presence among us illumined the path for countless souls, Paramahansa Yogananda lived and taught the highest truths of life. Born in Gorakhpur, India, in 1893, Paramahansa Yogananda was sent by his guru to the United States in 1920 as India's delegate to an International Congress of Religious Liberals. Subsequent lectures in Boston, New York, and Philadelphia were enthusiastically received, and in 1924 he embarked on a cross-continental speaking tour.

For the next decade Paramahansaji travelled extensively, giving lectures and classes in which he instructed thousands of men and women in the yoga science of meditation and balanced spiritual living.

Today, the spiritual and humanitarian work begun by Paramahansa Yogananda continues under the direction of Sri Sri Swami Chidananda Giri, president of Yogoda Satsanga Society of India/Self-Realization Fellowship. In addition to publishing Paramahansa Yogananda's writings, lectures, and informal talks (including a comprehensive series of *Yogoda Satsanga Lessons* for home study*), the society oversees ashrams, kendras, and meditation centres around the world; monastic training programs; and the Worldwide Prayer Circle, which serves as a channel to help bring healing to those in need and greater peace and harmony among all nations. Seekers in India and surrounding countries are served by Yogoda Satsanga Society of India.

* See page 114 for information about the *Yogoda Satsanga Lessons*.

In an article on Sri Yogananda's life and work, Quincy Howe, Jr., Ph. D., Professor of Ancient Languages, Scripps College, wrote: "Paramahansa Yogananda brought to the West not only India's perennial promise of God-realization, but also a practical method by which spiritual aspirants from all walks of life may progress rapidly toward that goal. Originally appreciated in the West only on the most lofty and abstract level, the spiritual legacy of India is now accessible as practice and experience to all who aspire to know God, not in the beyond, but in the here and now.... Yogananda has placed within the reach of all the most exalted methods of contemplation."

The life and teachings of Paramahansa Yogananda are described in his *Autobiography of a Yogi*. An award-winning documentary film about his life and work, *Awake: The Life of Yogananda,* was released in October 2014.

Paramahansa Yogananda: A Yogi in Life and Death

Sri Sri Paramahansa Yogananda entered *mahasamadhi* (a yogi's final conscious exit from the body) in Los Angeles, California, on March 7, 1952, after concluding his speech at a banquet held in honour of H.E. Binay R. Sen, Ambassador of India.

The great world teacher demonstrated the value of yoga (scientific techniques for God-realization) not only in life but in death. Weeks after his departure his unchanged face shone with the divine lustre of incorruptibility.

Mr. Harry T. Rowe, Los Angeles Mortuary Director, Forest Lawn Memorial-Park (in which the body of the great master is temporarily placed), sent Self-Realization Fellowship a notarized letter from which the following extracts are taken:

"The absence of any visual signs of decay in the dead body of Paramahansa Yogananda offers the most extraordinary case in our experience....No physical disintegration was visible in his body even twenty days after death.... No indication of mould was visible on his skin, and no visible desiccation (drying up) took place in the bodily tissues. This state of perfect preservation of a body is, so far as we know from mortuary annals, an unparalleled one....At the time of receiving Yogananda's body, the Mortuary personnel expected to observe, through the glass lid of the casket, the usual progressive signs of bodily decay. Our astonishment increased as day followed day without bringing any visible change in the body under observation. Yogananda's body was apparently in a phenomenal state of immutability....

"No odour of decay emanated from his body at any time....The physical appearance of Yogananda on March 27th, just before the bronze cover of the casket was put into position, was the same as it had been on March 7th. He looked on March 27th as fresh and as unravaged by decay as he had looked on the night of his death. On March 27th there was no reason to say that his body had suffered any visible physical disintegration at all. For these reasons we state again that the case of Paramahansa Yogananda is unique in our experience."

"O Father, I want prosperity, health, and wisdom without measure, not from earthly sources but from Thine all-possessing, all-powerful, all-bountiful hands."

—*Sri Sri Paramahansa Yogananda*

God lives in every atom of creation. If He withdrew His life-giving Presence, worlds would vanish tracelessly in the ether.

Man depends totally upon his Creator. Just as the health, happiness, and success he attracts result from his observance of God-ordained laws, so the help and healing he requires are attainable directly from God through prayer.

Prayers for healing of physical disease, mental inharmony, and spiritual ignorance are offered daily by Yogoda Satsanga Society of India/Self-Realization Fellowship monks and nuns. Through the blessings of God, thousands have received spiritual help.

You may request prayers for yourself or your loved ones by visiting our website, or by writing or telephoning:

YOGODA SATSANGA SOCIETY OF INDIA
Paramahansa Yogananda Path
Ranchi 834001, Jharkhand
Tel.: (0651) 6655 555
www.yssofindia.org

Yogoda Satsanga Lessons in Self-realization

Personal guidance and instruction from Paramahansa Yogananda on the techniques of yoga meditation and principles of spiritual living

If you feel drawn to the spiritual truths described in *Scientific Healing Affirmations,* we invite you to enrol in the *Yogoda Satsanga Lessons.*

Paramahansa Yogananda originated this home-study series to provide sincere seekers the opportunity to learn and practise the ancient yoga meditation techniques introduced in this book—including the science of *Kriya Yoga.* The *Lessons* also present his practical guidance for attaining balanced physical, mental and spiritual well-being.

The *Yogoda Satsanga Lessons* are available at a nominal fee (to cover printing and postage costs). All students are freely given personal guidance in their practice by Yogoda Satsanga Society of India monks.

For more information…

Please visit www.ysslessons.org to request a comprehensive complimentary information packet about the *Lessons,* which includes:

- *"An Overview of the Yogoda Satsanga Lessons in Self-realization: Information About Paramahansa Yogananda's Home-Study Series"*
- *"Highest Achievements Through Self-realization," by Paramahansa Yogananda—a thorough introduction to the teachings presented in the YSS Lessons*

Aims and Ideals
of
Yogoda Satsanga Society of India

As set forth by
Sri Sri Paramahansa Yogananda, Gurudeva and Founder
Sri Sri Swami Chidananda Giri, President

To disseminate among the nations a knowledge of definite scientific techniques for attaining direct personal experience of God.

To teach that the purpose of life is the evolution, through self-effort, of man's limited mortal consciousness into God Consciousness; and to this end to establish Yogoda Satsanga temples for God-communion, and to encourage the establishment of individual temples of God in the homes and in the hearts of men.

To reveal the complete harmony and basic oneness of original Yoga as taught by Bhagavan Krishna and original Christianity as taught by Jesus Christ; and to show that these principles of truth are the common scientific foundation of all true religions.

To point out the one divine highway to which all paths of true religious beliefs eventually lead: the highway of daily, scientific, devotional meditation on God.

To liberate man from his threefold suffering: physical disease, mental inharmonies, and spiritual ignorance.

To encourage "plain living and high thinking;" and to spread a spirit of brotherhood among all peoples by teaching the eternal basis of their unity: kinship with God.

To demonstrate the superiority of mind over body, of soul over mind.

To overcome evil by good, sorrow by joy, cruelty by kindness, ignorance by wisdom.

To unite science and religion through realization of the unity of their underlying principles.

To advocate cultural and spiritual understanding between East and West, and the exchange of their finest distinctive features.

To serve mankind as one's larger Self.

Other Books by
Sri Sri Paramahansa Yogananda

Available at bookstores or online at bookstore.yssofindia.org

Autobiography of a Yogi

Autobiography of a Yogi
(Audiobook, read by Sir Ben Kingsley)

God Talks With Arjuna: The Bhagavad Gita—
A New Translation and Commentary

The Second Coming of Christ:
The Resurrection of the Christ Within You—
A Revelatory Commentary
on the Original Teachings of Jesus

The Collected Talks and Essays
Volume I: Man's Eternal Quest
Volume II: The Divine Romance
Volume III: Journey to Self-realization

Wine of the Mystic: The Rubaiyat of Omar Khayyam—
A Spiritual Interpretation

The Science of Religion

Whispers from Eternity

Songs of the Soul

Sayings of Paramahansa Yogananda

Metaphysical Meditations

Where There Is Light: Insight and Inspiration for
Meeting Life's Challenges

In the Sanctuary of the Soul:
A Guide to Effective Prayer

Inner Peace:
How to Be Calmly Active and Actively Calm

Living Fearlessly:
Bringing Out Your Inner Soul Strength

Why God Permits Evil and How to Rise Above It

How You Can Talk With God

Prayers of a Master for His Disciples

To Be Victorious in Life

The Law of Success

Words of Cosmic Chants

Some of the above-mentioned books are also published in Hindi, Assamese, Bengali, Gujarati, Kannada, Malayalam, Marathi, Nepali, Odia, Punjabi, Sanskrit, Sinhala, Tamil, Telugu, and Urdu. For a complete list of books and audio/video recordings visit our online store at the address given below. Also available are black-and-white and colour pictures of Sri Sri Paramahansa Yogananda.

Available at your local bookstore or from:

YOGODA SATSANGA SOCIETY OF INDIA
Paramahansa Yogananda Path
Ranchi 834001, Jharkhand
Tel.: (0651) 6655 555

www.yssbooks.org

INDEX